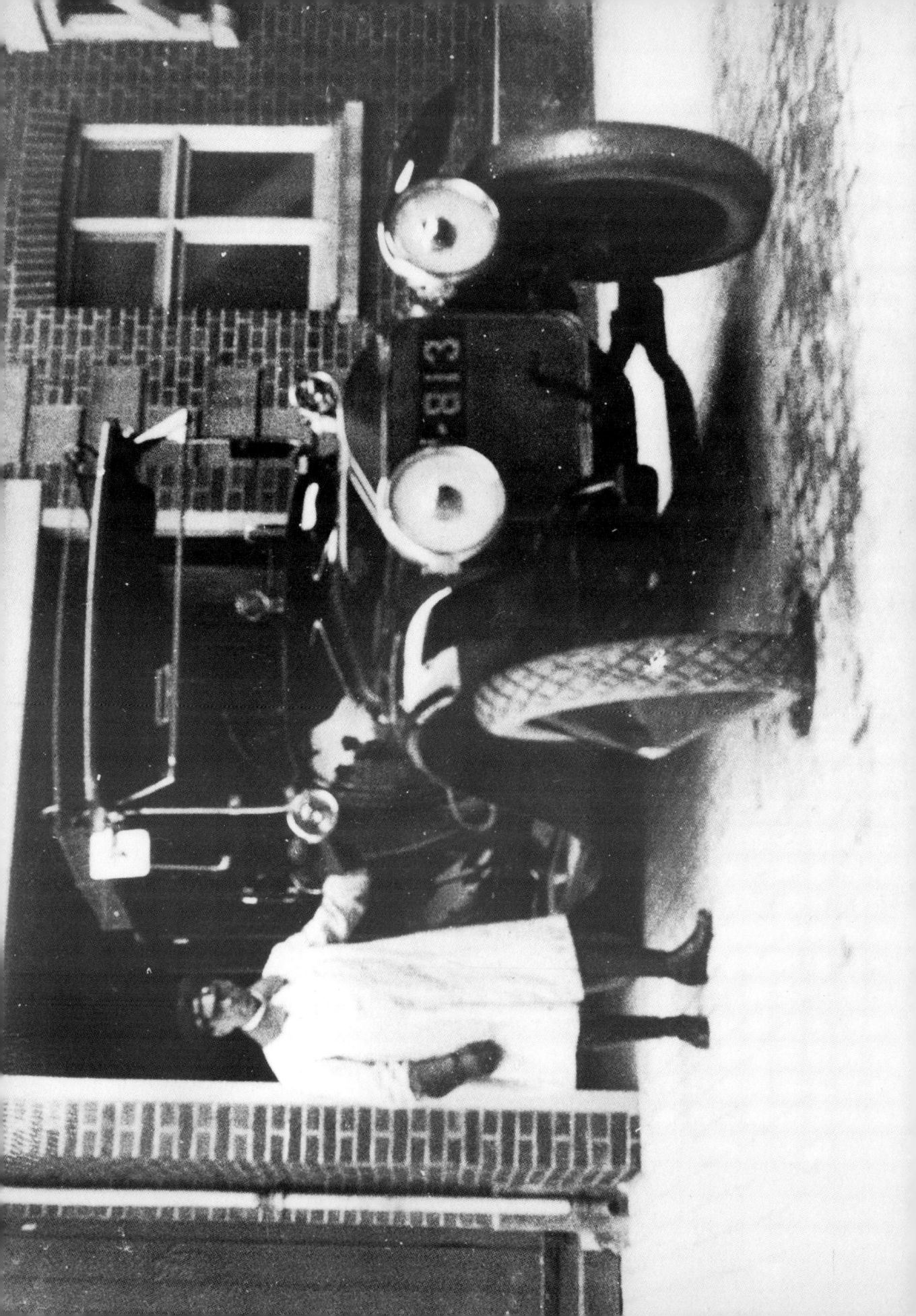

The Vanishing Villas of Preston & Withdean

compiled by Selma Montford, Jacqueline Pollard and Robert Sanderson

CONTENTS
The Development of the Villas in Preston & Withdean 1
Preston Villa 5
`Norbury 5
Grove Lodge and St John's 6
Woodslee 9
Cliveden 9
Withdeane Lodge 11
Hatch Beauchamp 12
Fir Croft, Laine House and Effingham Lodge 12
Withdeane Hall 14
Map of Withdean 16 & 17
Withdean Court 18
Miramichi, Withdean Grange and Tramore 19
Lea Hurst 19
Beechwood 20
Elms Lea 21
Tivoli 23
Tower House 25
Below Stairs in the Withdean Villas 27
The Preston Park Villas 31

Cover: Rossmore 127 Preston Road c.1912
Front end papers: Withdeane Lodge c.1913
Opposite: chauffeur at Elms Lea in the 1920s

Brighton Books
Publishing

HIGH(?) ROAD, PRESTON.

The Development of the Villas of Withdean and Preston

Introduction

Brighton was pressing against its parish boundaries by 1861, and was so short of building land that speculators were seeking sites for building houses at some distance from the town's boundaries. This fashionable resort had one of the highest urban population densities in the United Kingdom. Villas, the most prestigious form of town housing, could only be inland at a distance from the town - at Withdean to the north of Brighton, or well to the west of the Brunswick Town Estate in the parish of Hove.[1]

The villas of Withdean were very special when they were built, as they were set in spacious grounds, unique in the vicinity of Brighton. The reason for the extensive grounds was that land was cheaper owing to its distance from the town centre. The villas which fringed Preston Park, built to the south of Preston from the 1870s, lacked spacious grounds, but had the advantages of being closer to the town centre and the proximity to Preston Park after its development by Brighton Council.

In this study, the development of both groups of villas will be set into the context of the growth of Brighton and Hove.

The context

By 1861 Brighton was surrounded by land which was not available for building. All the land to the north and west of the town which was suitable for development, because it was either low lying and by the sea, or along the main roads leading northwards out of the town, was owned by the Stanford family, and it was not sold until 1871. To the east of Brighton steep slopes to the racecourse inhibited development, and along the coast the Abergavenny estate in the parish of Rottingdean, which abutted on to Brighton, was prospering as farmland. The cliffs made access to the sea impractical.[2]

As the Stanfords' land was not available, the solution was to build beyond it to the north or west. Only those who could afford the travel costs to the town could afford such locations, even after suburban railway stations were opened, as people were very conscious of the costs of travel. This was why villas were built where they were as there seemed to be a market for them, rather than use the land for cheaper housing.

In 1853 the Trustees of the stretch of turnpike road which began at the southern end of Preston village and continued northwards applied to Parliament for the renewal of their powers. A group of influential people from Brighton and Preston were successful in getting the tollgate removed to the north. In May 1854, the gate was moved a hundred yards north of Withdean. This action improved the prospects for those who wished to sell or to buy land for development in Preston and Withdean, because residents who used the road to Brighton would not have to pay a toll. Amongst the beneficiaries of the resited tollgate were the proprietors of the Strawberry Gardens, who improved them and renamed them the Tivoli Gardens in 1852. So it was at Withdean (in the parish of Patcham) that building began after 1853.[3]

Opposite: London Road looking north c.1910. The finger post points up Clermont Road to Preston Park Station.

Withdean was not the only villa project which was being developed beyond the boundaries of Brighton by the mid 1850s, in order to meet the need for new houses. Cliftonville was also being built, but it was a more truly suburban project planned by a group of speculators. Withdean developed in a piecemeal fashion with more upmarket houses. When studying the development of the villas of northern Brighton, it is important to remember that they were meeting the demand for luxury accommodation without sea views, whereas the coastal plain in Hove was being developed for people who sought proximity to the sea.[4]

Beginnings

One of the delights of Withdean was its ready-made wooded landscape, a legacy from an enthusiastic amateur landscape gardener called William Roe.[5] From the early 1850s, Eliza Roe (who married Sir Charles Ogle), sold land which had been part of the Roe estate in Withdean. This sale provided land for development on both sides of the London Road north of Preston (see map centre pages), and by 1851 development had begun. Mrs Helen Madden, the wife of a physician, was listed as the head of a large household at Woodslee, and nearby was a half finished house. A furrier from the City of London (George Riddlestaff) with his family and staff were resident in the vicinity of Withdean in 1851, but the house was not named in the census. In 1851, John Rogers and Robert Ayling occupied Withdean Strawberry Gardens, which they renamed Tivoli Gardens soon after the census of 1851. One result of the sale of land was that the rest of the Roe Estate was reorganised into new farms.[6]

Between 1851 and 1861 more large houses were built between the hamlet of Withdean and Preston village. By 1861 the east side of the road had several villas lining it: Grove Lodge was occupied by a retired wine merchant; and St. John's Villa by the Clarence sisters, who ran a private boarding school with 20 girls in residence. Farther north, Woodslee (occupied by a barrister); Hartford Villa and Withdeane Hall (of 1861 and described soon after as a handsome Elizabethan building) were all occupied; and Elizabeth Ogle, widow, lived in Withdean Court. The land to the west of London Road had not been developed, but the Tivoli Gardens still flourished. By 1869 the east side was being infilled and the west side was also being developed; the villas included Stamford Villa, Miramachi and the Laurels. Additional villas on the east side of the London Road included Effingham Lodge and Fir Croft. St. John's had become St. John's Hall Ladies School.[7] A wide variety of architectural styles were used, ranging from Victorian Gothic to Queen Anne Revival, in addition to more traditional classical villa designs.

By 1871 a Baptist Chapel with a school had been built at Withdean, Stamford Villa had been renamed Terrick Cottage and Laine House had been built. Elizabeth Ogle had built a new house just north of the present Withdean Court Avenue and took the name of her previous house, Withdean Court with her; while her previous house became the Old Court House. The Tivoli Gardens survived until 1888 when the land was purchased by the owner of Elms Lee (Mr R C Gazeley).[8]

The Ogle's land was inherited by the Curwen family who continued to sell it for development. They named the Surrenden area after Surrenden Hall in Kent where Eliza Roe's mother had lived.[9]

Whilst Withdean was being turned into a little hamlet of villas, the development of the Clermont Estate commenced, built on land which was sold by William Harrington,

Norbury adjoining Preston Villa in 1923, now the Jarvis Preston Park Hotel.

stretching from the northern end of Preston village to the parish boundary with Patcham.[10] The Clermont estate, originally planned for 200 houses, was promoted by Daniel Friend (who promoted Prestonville) in 1866 when building began. The Clermont Estate was intended for people who could afford to take cabs or carriages to work or (from 1869) to take the train. These large, mainly terraced or semi-detached houses, most of which were rented, offered clean air and spacious gardens to upper middle class people. In 1871, Clermont Terrace was still being built and there were eight houses in Clermont Villas.[11]

Just as the building of the Clermont Estate was drawing to a close, the land south of Preston village down to the boundary with Brighton came on to the market. The Stanford Estate was made available for building in 1871, when Ellen Stanford reached the age of 21, her father William having died when she was young. The sale of land on the estate from 1871 onwards enabled Brighton to burst its boundaries to the north and to the west. The character of the building projects which the Stanford Estate permitted in Preston were clearly different from those which it accepted on the land in Hove, which was by the sea. Inland, most of the development was for lower middle and middle class residents who wanted houses, while a prestigious seaside project was drawn up for the land in Hove.[12]

The Stanford Estate in Preston developed as a popular middle class suburb, with open spaces, generous road layouts, and decorative features on many of the houses. The peak of building in Preston was between 1876 and 1900, with some infilling from 1921-25. The most expensive houses were the detached villas, most of which were in the valley bottom close to the London Road, or along Stanford Avenue, the main road through the centre of the estate which connects the London Road to the Ditchling Road. The Stanfords did not develop the parks themselves - Hove and Preston Parks and Hove Recreation Ground were developed by Brighton and Hove Councils respectively. The land for Preston Park was sold to Brighton Council in the 1890s, following an earlier unsuccessful attempt to do so.[13]

The design of each villa, the minimum building costs, and the time which was taken to get the property constructed, were all controlled by the Stanford Estate by conditions in the conveyances from them to the developer. Most of the villas were constructed by speculative builders who hoped to sell the property on. This is a contrast with Withdean where the purchasers were normally people who intended to live there and who then commissioned the building.[14]

The cost of land and the minimum building costs which the Stanfords laid down depended upon the location of the site and the size of the plot. Terraced houses in streets such as Chester Terrace had to cost at least £350 to build. A villa in Preston Park Avenue had to cost at least £600 in the late 1880s, and in 1883 a group along the west side of Preston Park had to cost at least £1,500 each to construct. Development was not allowed to take place in a piecemeal fashion, land was released in an orderly manner, mainly from the south of the estate northwards towards Preston Manor, the Stanford family home.[15]

By 1900 London Road from the boundary with Brighton to the north of Withdean was built up. Only one of the three key landowners, the Stanfords, played any role in deciding what should be built; while the Harrington and Ogle families did not. The attractive setting, combined with the cost of access to the town centre dictated that villas would be one of the key characteristics of all of the suburban building which took place. Their legacy is still visible in the landscape of today and offers a scattering of architectural details and set in a distinctive treescape for those who are willing to wander about on foot.[16] (References inside back cover).

Sue Berry

Preston Villa built for Nathaniel Blaker in 1853. View from the back garden in 1907.

LONDON ROAD - EAST SIDE

Preston Villa, 1 Harrington Road

Preston Villa was built on land described in Henry Smithers will of 1772 as Kenyeo Farm. It was commisioned by a widower Nathaniel Blaker in 1853. He originally lived there with his daughters Anna and May. He remarried fairly soon afterwards and his daughters stayed at the villa until 1864 when May married. Anna remained there until her death in the 1880's aged 74, leaving Preston Villa to her nephew Nathaniel Paine Blaker. In 1893 it was sold to Caroline Emma Willoughby, and the north wing was added to accommodate her two daughters. Caroline died in 1898, and the villa was sold in 1900 to Thomas John Groves who, with his son Alfred, ran a laundry business and had stables built in the gardens for their horses. Alfred died in 1948 and the house was divided between the eldest and youngest daughters. The east and west wings were sold as separate houses in the 1960's. Part of the garden, including the orchard, was sold for building at this time, but in spite of attempts to incorporate the villa into the hotel, the villa remains in private ownership.

Norbury (photograph page 3)

Norbury, originally called Selborne, was a large villa built on London Road and attached to Preston Villa in Harrington Road. It was lived in by the Berryman family in the 20's and 30's until 1934 when road widening took much of the front garden, so they moved to Tower House. The house was sold and became Methuen Manor Nursing Home until the 1960's when it was changed into The Touring Hotel. It has remained a hotel, and is now called The Jarvis Preston Park Hotel. Although many alterations and extensions have been made to the original building the south facing facade is intact.

The lodge of Grove Lodge 1902, at the entrance to the present St Bernadette's Roman Catholic Primary School. Grove Lodge itself can be seen in the distance. Today the lodge is much closer to London Road, due to road widening in the 1930s.

Grove Lodge

Grove Lodge, a smaller house than many of its neighbours, was built in the 1860's on the east side of London Road, in between the much grander villas of Norbury and St John's. Francis Brown, a retired wine merchant, was the first occupant of Grove Lodge, which remained a private house until the 1950's when it was badly damaged by fire and was purchased by the Sisters of Christian Instruction from Nevers in France. It was rebuilt and became part of Lourdes Convent. Today, much altered and extended, it is part of St. Bernadettes Roman Catholic Primary School. Grove Lodge's lodge is still visible from the Preston Road. (photograph page 5)

Pupils at Lourdes Convent near the verandah of St John's House in 1922. The corrugated iron chapel is in the background.

St. John's Villa

St. John's Villa first appears on the 1861 census showing Emma Clarence aged 59, running a Seminary for Young Ladies. It is said that the house had originally been a boys' school and the owner named it St. John's after his college at Oxford.

Emma Clarence was assisted in the running of the school by her sister Suzanne until 1870 when, with ailing health, they asked their widowed sister in South Africa to return and help them. Sarah Jane Visick took over the school in 1870, but she died aged 46 in 1876 leaving her daughter Emma to run the school.

St. John's was a large Regency style Italianate villa, standing well back from the London Road, in an old-world garden. Established trees bordered the road and near the front door were cedars, a tulip tree and a copper beech. Young ladies did not play games in those days, apart from a little gentle croquet, and certainly nobody was allowd to run, which would have been difficult anyway in their restrictive clothes. Therefore a great deal of time was spent walking, reading or sewing in the garden, or tending small plots which were alloted to pupils. The kitchen garden was full of fruit, but was out of bounds. There were swings and a see-saw in a small enclosure and two summer houses were sometimes used for tea parties. The house itself was large and comfortable and the schoolrooms had thick carpets and curtains. There were tables with tapestry cloths, but no desks, the chairs were small and hard, and the pupils' beds were similarly spartan. In each of the larger rooms a corner was curtained off for a teacher.

The Studio at Lourdes Convent

Everyone rose at 6.30 am summer and winter, and lessons started at 7 am. This must have been by candle light in winter as gas had not been installed in the 1870s. At 8 am the girls repeated texts and sang a hymn. Breakfast followed, then a short walk in warm shawls and galoshes. The main meal of the day was at 2 pm, followed by another walk, in normal outdoor wear, with tea at 6 pm. Biscuits and cold water were set out at bedtime. On Sundays cold meat was served, to allow the servants to have some much needed time off.

The teaching at St. John's was considered suitable for young ladies. Spelling was learnt every day, as was mental arithmetic and geography, with rote learning of dates. There was a French and German governess in the early years, but later French was taught by a visiting master, French conversation was compulsory. The census shows us that the average number at the school was 28 pupils, the majority being between 13-17 years old, although there were occasionally also younger pupils. There were five domestic servants to cater for the pupils, a cook and a wardrobe mistress. The academic staff consisted of the principal, deputy and three governesses living in the school, as well as visiting tutors.

In 1903, The Sisters of Christian Instruction from Nevers in France took over the school and by 1901 it was known as Lourdes Convent. They built a chapel in the grounds which was elaborately rebuilt in 1938 in a Gothic design by J S Gilbert. In the 1920's they purchased Woodslee, a large villa to the north of St John's, and linked the two houses with a covered corridor. The beautiful front gardens of the two houses were converted into tennis courts at this time and, with the purchase of Grove Lodge in the 1950's, the school numbers reached 400 pupils, both day and boarding.

In the early 1970's there was a reorganisation of Roman Catholic schools in the area and Lourdes Convent closed and became part of Cardinal Newman School. The buildings, including the chapel, were demolished in 1972, leaving Grove Lodge to continue as St Bernadette's Roman Catholic Middle school a year later. The sites of St John's and Woodslee were then sold to developers who erected Kingsmere flats. Some of the beautiful trees from the original gardens survive today thanks to efforts of the Preston Society.

Convent of the Sisters of Nevers

Opposite: Convent of the Sisters of Nevers, School House.

Woodslee

Woodslee was one of the first villas to be built in London Road, appearing on the 1851 census, with Helen Maddon aged 31, the wife of a physician in residence. Between 1871 and the early 1900's Charles Armstrong, a retired shop merchant, and his family lived there. Bruce Morison then owned the house until the early 1920's when it was bought by The Sisters of Christian Instruction to form part of Lourdes Convent school. It was demolished in 1972 and Kingsmere flats now stand on the site.

Tennis courts in front of Lourdes Convent in the early 1930s. St John's is showing above the trees.

Cliveden

Cliveden was built in the 1850s, similar to its neighbour to the south, but with an impressive palm house on its north side, and surrounded by about three acres of land. It was originally called Hartford Villa and later Springfield Villa. Its lodge on London Road was built later than the main house, which was built in 1885 in Victorian Elizabethan style. Cliveden was demolished in the early 1960's, however its lodge survives today at the entrance to the blocks of flats, appropriately named Cliveden Court, built on the site.

Edward and Alice Norris in front of Withdeane Lodge in 1913.

Edward Norris with one of his daughters in the garden of Withdeane Lodge in 1913.

The Round House in 1913, it can be seen today, still with a conservatory in the roof.

Withdeane Lodge

Withdeane Lodge, built in the 1860s, was typical of the Regency style Italianate villas in Withdean (see front endpapers), with six bedrooms, four reception rooms and the usual domestic offices in the basement: kitchen, scullery, butler's pantry, knife house, store rooms and wine cellar. Brick and flint boundary walls enclosed well timbered grounds of about four acres with orchard, kitchen garden, greenhouses, coachhouse, stable-block and vinery. The endpapers show the veranda overlooking the garden, with a carriage drive from London Road, where the Round House, marked the entrance to the grounds.

From the 1860's the house was owned by five sisters, the Misses Gregory. In 1884 Maria and Juliana Gregory founded the Sussex Temporary Home for Lost and Starving Dogs on the corner of Millers and Robertson Roads, in memory of their sister Caroline (see page 12). A commemorative plaque can be seen on the original red brick and flint house in Robertson Road; the main site is now occupied by the PDSA. When Juliana Gregory died in 1897, her remaining sisters erected a drinking fountain, in London Road opposite Tongdean Lane, as a memorial to her. It was later moved north to Patcham, where it can be seen today at the junction with the Old London Road.

Withdeane Lodge was bought from the Gregorys in 1907 for £4,500 by Edward James Norris, a wealthy property owner, architect and surveyor. Before moving in he instructed the builders, Penfold of 219 Preston Road, to carry out alterations and repairs costing £1,321, including renovation of the glasshouses and demolition of the coach house to be replaced by a motor garage, with inspection pit.

Edward Norris and his son Stanley, shared the Edwardian gentleman's passion for collecting antiquities, and used part of the house as a library and private museum. This contained many fascinating exhibits, including ancient Greek and Roman pottery, fossils, minerals, arms and armour, ethnographical specimens and items from ancient Egypt. Edward Norris died in 1930, his wife Alice stayed on at the house until her death a decade later, when Withdeane Lodge was sold.

During World War II the house was occupied by troops and then split into flats. Finally at the beginning of the 1960's it was demolished, as was the neighbouring Cliveden. The site was developed with Grosvenor Court and Cliveden Court flats. The Round House escaped demolition as did the stable-block and vinery.

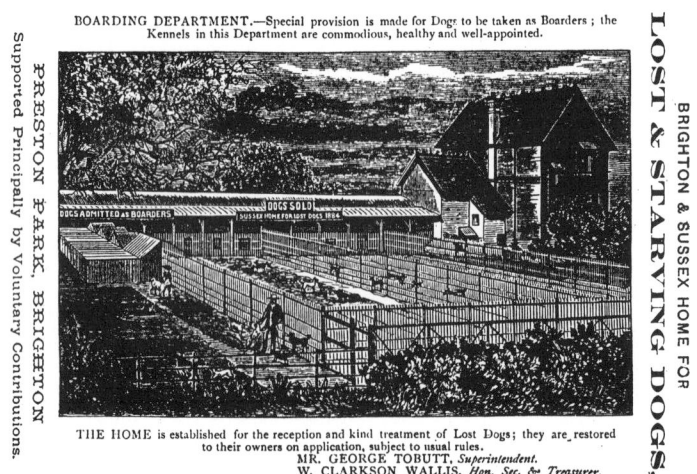

Hatch Beauchamp

Hatch Beauchamp, originally called Withdean House, was built c.1870 north of Varndean Road in grounds of three and a half acres. Its lodge on the London Road is now the only clue to its existence, as the main house was demolished in 1937, when blocks of flats called Withdean Court were erected on the site.

Fir Croft, Effingham Lodge and Laine House

Fir Croft, Effingham Lodge and Laine House, were built in the late 1850's or early 1860's, each in two acre grounds. The Italianate Fir Croft was the largest of the Regency style houses in the area, and for many years was home to the Misses Davison. It had two lodges, one on London Road and another, Fir Croft Cottage, half-way up Varndean Road.

Comparitively, Effingham Lodge was rather a plain house with a conservatory, billiard room and grounds containing croquet and tennis lawns. For many years home to the Bates family, in 1928 Mr Bates offered a fortnight's work as a cook to a Mrs Wagstaff (see photograph page 28) - she accepted and stayed on with the family for 28 years!

Laine House was built in Victorian Gothic style, with two conservatories, and a lodge cottage on the London Road built in the same gothic style as the main house.

These three adjoining properties, along with Fir Croft Cottage, were purchased by Brighton Corporation between 1956 and 1972 at £131,350. In 1954 the Corporation had already acquired three and a half acres behind these houses at a cost of £500, assembling a site of ten acres. This land was sold lease-hold to developers for £1,026,000, at a profit of £894,150, hence the nickname for the site: 'Golden Acres'. Brighton Corporation put the proceeds of the sale of this site towards the cost of its Conference Centre in King's Road.

The developers demolished the three old houses and their lodges, and built an estate of 164 flats and houses, the only acknowledgement of the previous properties in the name of two roads on the estate, Fir Croft Close and Laine Close. The Preston Society campaigned successfully for the retention of most of the trees on the site.

Laine House c.1910, the home of Thomas Jerrard at this time.

Effingham Lodge about the turn of the century.

Withdeane Hall in the early 20s, now converted into flats. Note the palm house now demolished.

Withdeane Hall

Withdeane Hall was built in Victorian Elizabethan style in 1861. Red brick and flint were used to decorate its ornate facade and central chimney stack, while an incongruous viewing platform was built in the patterned roof. On the north side of the building was a large domed palm house, accessible from the garden and the main house via a long glass corridor. The Hall stood in many acres of grounds with two old farm cottages to the east. At its entrance gates on the London Road a two storied lodge, built in the same extravagant style as the Hall was home to a gardener, while the old farm cottages were used as stables and coachman's accommodation.

In 1876 the house was bought by the Rt Hon Sir Francis Mowatt (Secretary to the Treasury 1894-1903). He had six children by his wife Lucy, but also a stepson, Count Eric Stenbock. Although born near Cheltenham in 1859, Eric Stenbock inherited vast estates in Estonia (which had been in his father's family since the 18th century) in 1885, but spent much of his life in England. A writer of dark and morbid poetry, he became an acquaintance of Yeats and Oscar Wilde, and was renowned for his eccentric and hedonistic behaviour. Curiously, a Stenbock family story says that Frank Mowatt presented his stepson to Queen Victoria, who was so pleased with him that she often sent for him.

By the early 1890's however, his decadent lifestyle had begun to take its toll, and his health deteriorated badly, aggravated by his alcoholism. At Withdeane Hall, Count Stenbock, mentally as well as physically ill, terrified staff and the young Mowatt children with his delirium. He also insisted on being accompanied on his travels by a dog, a smelly monkey, and a life-size doll. He was convinced the doll was his son and referred to it as 'le Petit Comte'.

The end came for the Count on 26 April 1895. Apparently drunk and furious, he had tried to strike someone with a poker and toppled into a fire-grate. Later that day he died. He was buried in the Brighton Catholic Cemetery 'in the presence (said the Brighton Examiner) of a large number of relatives and friends.' Before the burial, his heart was extracted and sent to Estonia, where it was preserved in some fluid in a glass urn, and placed among the Stenbock monuments in the church at Kursal.

After the Mowatts left at the turn of the century, Withdeane Hall had a number of different owners until the 1930's when it became K F Robinson's Preparatory School for Boys. Around this time Varndean Gardens and Withdean Crescent were developed on either side of the house, merging in front of the building. The Approach was constructed to link them with London Road.

During World War II the Hall was used as a billet for troops. After this it stood empty for sometime, before eventually being sold by the Ministry of Health in 1950 for a reported £2,800. It was then converted into ten flats.

It seems sad that many of the interesting exterior details such as the tower, tall chimney stacks, crow-stepped gable ends and other Victorian Elizabethan touches have been removed over the years. It is sad that when it was converted into flats more time was not spent blending the old with the new on the facade. However at least the building survives today, as do the cottages at the back and its lodge on the London Road. Sadly the great palm house was lost sometime after the 1930's.

Withdean Hall Lodge 1924. Mrs Langstone, cook and wife of the gardener lived there. It is still standing.

Withdean Court shortly after it was built in 1871. Photograph courtesy Clayton, Black & Daviel archive

LONDON ROAD - WEST SIDE

Withdean Court

Withdean Court was commissioned by Lady Eliza Ogle, granddaughter of William Roe and heir to the Withdean Estate, and built in 1871 by J Parsons & Sons of Hove. The architects were Clayton, Black and Daviel of Brighton, who designed the house in Victorian Gothic style, rare in Brighton.

It was the largest of all the grand villas built in Withdean, stood in several acres, with an entrance lodge on the London Road, and at one time a chapel. Lady Ogle also had a small school built in the grounds for the children of her employees, to whom she also gave free use of some of her land as allotments.

On the death of Lady Ogle in 1886 the house passed to her daughter Hebe, who was married to Eldred Curwen. Sadly Hebe Curwen died just three years after her mother in 1889, but Eldred lived on at Withdean Court until his death in 1927. The house was then sold and converted into eight separate flats, and renamed Dene Court. Around this time some of the grounds were sold for housing, and for Withdean Court Avenue.

In the 1930's Dene Court flats were bought by Baron Willie von Pantzer, who renamed them Pantzer Mansions. Willie Pantzer was a naturalised British citizen, but a descendant of a family of armourers from Nuremberg, Germany from whom he inherited his title. He was a well known variety artist and showman, who regularly travelled abroad with his acts, known as the Pantzer Troop who lived in the flats at Pantzer Mansions. He provided a gymnasium in the grounds for their training. The Baron let out the lodge cottage on the London Road as The Rendezvous Cafe, while he and his wife and son lived in a house in the grounds called the Manor, similar in appearance to the main house, but smaller.

Baron Willie Von Pantzer died in the early 1960's, the Mansions and grounds were then sold to developers, who demolished all the buildings and erected Regency Court and Park Manor Flats on the site.

Miramichi, Withdean Grange and Tramore

The next three houses going south were Miramichi, Withdean Grange built in the 1860s, and Tramore built in the 1890s. Miramichi stood in over two acres of land, with a lodge on London Road. Its grounds were developed as Cedars Gardens in about 1932, but the house itself survived, later renamed The Cedars. In the early 1980s The Cedars was demolished and replaced by flats. Its lodge remains at the entrance to Cedars Gardens.

Withdean Grange, originally named Stamford Villa, then Terrick Cottage, was set in four acres of land planted with many rare trees. There was a lodge at its entrance and at the back of the house a stable yard, with a tall clock tower on the roof. For many years Withdean Grange was home to F F Flinn of Flinn's Ltd, the dry cleaners with shops throughout Brighton and Hove. In the 1950s the house was bought by British Telecom, for use as a telephone exchange. Over the years modern buildings were erected on the site and the old house, stables and lodge were demolished. Sadly most of the trees have disappeared.

Tramore was built on a thin strip of land which probably once belonged to Lea Hurst, its southerly neighbour. It was small in comparison with most of the Withdean houses, but big enough to be split into flats in the 1950s. Tramore was demolished in the 1970s and the site developed with flats and houses.

Lea Hurst

Originally called The Laurels and built in the 1860s, Lea Hurst was a large red brick house boasting 12 bedrooms and four acres of grounds. A good description is given in sale particulars issued in 1907 by Maple & Co, Land and Estate Agents, King's Road, Brighton.

'Sussex, Brighton. Situated about five minutes walk from Preston Park Station, 2 miles from the sea and close to church, post and telegraph office, an exceedingly well-built Family Residence, standing in its own well-timbered and secluded grounds of 4 acres, approached by a carriage drive with entrance lodge, and gardener's cottage, and containing-on the top floor, six bedrooms, dressing room, bathroom with hot and cold supplies, lavatory and wc; on the first floor, 4 large bedrooms, dressing room, bathroom with hot and cold supplies, lavatory, hot linen closet and wc, also separate landing with 2 servants' bedrooms; on the ground floor, a handsome lounge, hall with fitted fireplace, drawing, dining and morning rooms, conservatory (with entrance from hall and dining room), leading into a very fine billiard room, lavatory, cloakroom; the domestic offices, which are on the same level, but completely shut off, include kitchen, scullery, servants' hall, butler's pantry, larder, stove cupboard etc; in the basement is a study, large room, wine cellars, &c. Stabling for two horses, coachhouse, harness room, &c. The pleasure grounds, which are tastefully laid out, include tennis lawn, flower beds and borders, very large kitchen garden and paddock, the whole covering an area of about 4 acres. Gas and water laid on throughout and drainage is good. The residence is in perfect order, and fitted with every modern convenience. Price: freehold £8,500.'

From 1928-1946 the house belonged to the Kingston family. Charles Kingston J P butcher and Mayor of Brighton in 1927, his daughters married into the Vokins family who lived next door in Beechwood. Lea Hurst was used as headquarters for 3701 (County of Sussex) Royal Auxiliary Air Force Radar Unit from 1953-1958. In 1959 it was sold at auction for £47,500, demolished, and the site developed as Lea Hurst Court flats.

Beechwood

Beechwood was a substantial red brick house, built in 1877 for Thomas Martin, set in three acres with vegetable garden, glasshouses, coachhouse, stables and a summer house. It was home to William Henry Vokins and family, owners of the local department store, from the early part of the century to 1956. In the late 1950's Beechwood was sold and then demolished, providing the site for Curwen Place flats.

Beechwood between the wars, home for many years to the Vokins family.

Mrs Vokins at Beechwood, between 1914 and '18, entertains wounded soldiers from WW1 and their families. The hosting of garden parties during the Great War was popular with the town's fashionable ladies.

Elms Lea c.1930, sold for development in 1934, now the site of Elms Lea Avenue

Elms Lea

Elms Lea was a fine house containing eight bed and dressing rooms, four reception rooms, billiard room, conservatory and domestic offices. Built in the 1870's it stood in attractive grounds of four acres, consisting of a field, tennis court, kitchen garden, stables, glass houses and a cottage.

One of its earliest owners was R C Gazeley, who was also the purchaser in 1888 of the Tivoli Pleasure Gardens, situated directly to the south of Elms Lea. Later this land became the site of Tower House and Tivoli.

At the turn of the century Elms Lea was bought by Leonard Bloomfield, head of a famous firm of military cap and helmet makers. He was a bibliophile, and on his death in December 1916 he bequeathed his collection of over 13,000 books, prints and early manuscripts, and a large part of the personal library of the poet Robert Browning and his wife Elizabeth Barrett Browning (purchased at Sotheby's in 1913) to Brighton Library.

The next owner of the house was Thomas Ronald, a partner in the Ritz Hotel in London, chairman of the Canadian Pacific Railway, and owner of consolidated fisheries at Grimsby and Swansea. He and his wife Annie had thirteen children, three of whom, Mary, Kathy and Madeleine lived with them at Elms Lea. Mary and Kathy were unmarried, but Madeleine's husband, John Reilley, and their children, Pamela and Patricia, also lived at the house. Patricia, still a resident of Brighton, recalls life at the house in the 1920's and early '30's.

" I remember four gardeners, Denton, Scutt, Scarfield and Mr Garnett the head gardener, who lived in the cottage above the stables. Booty the chauffeur wore a grey uniform and drove the maroon and black Daimler. I used to go for a ride in it most afternoons with my grandmother. I remember the cook, Doris the house maid, Ivy the scullery maid and Ethel the parlour maid, who rang the gong for meals. Lilly was my nursemaid. Then there was

The bride Madeleine, daughter of Mr and Mrs Thomas Ronald, on the occasion of her marriage to John Reilley on 8 January 1918 on the steps of Elms Lea.

my nanny, I think her Christian name was Gertrude, but we always called her Nanny Johnson. Nanny would take me to Preston Park and sometimes we would meet her friend Nanny Foster, with her employer's child. I remember watching polo in the park, and going round Rookery Nook. There was great love between me and Nanny, as I saw her more than I did my mother who was always out shopping, entertaining, or playing tennis. My father was an army officer in World War I and went on to serve in World War II as well; between the wars he was in the reserve. In 1926, when I was six months old, my grandfather died, so father took over the management of the Elms Lea estate.

The grounds of Elms Lea were beautiful with lots of fruit trees and two pampas grasses in the middle of the front lawn, and a grass tennis court where we had tennis parties in summer. Running along the length of the court was the rockery, and by the side my hammock and a revolving summer house, rather unusual in those days. There was a huge vegetable garden and there were dozens of chickens. A cow called Mumsie lived in the field. There had been hay making and stacking in the field, but that was before my time.

Inside the house was the hall with a tiled floor, and a grand staircase; another smaller staircase led from the hall to the basement with the kitchen, scullery, store rooms, wine cellars and walk-in larders with stone floors to help them keep cool. A man would come regularly with a block of ice on his back for the fridge - a little wooden box. In the basement was a servants' staircase, which led up the back of the house to the rooms in the roof, where Ethel, Doris and Ivy slept.

The drawing room was beautiful, with a parquet floor, grand piano, and lots of cabinets filled with glass and china. The furniture was in a Chinese style, with gilt and silk upholstery, and Chinese rugs on the floor. We were allowed into the drawing room only on very special occasions, and always accompanied by an adult.

The dining room was at the front of the house, and had a food lift from the basement, called the dumb waiter. On the sideboards were big silver tureens, and beautiful wooden boxes containing the silver cutlery. In the centre of the room was a big dining table. Granny always sat at the top in a big chair, and woe betide anyone who misbehaved! She was a typical Victorian, and always wore dark grey or black woolly dresses and a broach. At the side of the house was a little morning room which Granny used, it had a lovely fireplace and we had tea there in the afternoons. Off this was the conservatory with a vine and potted plants. The billiard room had wood-panelled walls with paintings of hunting scenes, a full sized billiard table, and two pianolas - my sister played the smaller one. At Christmas the tree would be in here, it was always right up to the ceiling and beautifully decorated. On Christmas day, before we had our presents, the servants would be given theirs off the tree, they also had their Christmas lunch before ours, served in their own sitting room by my parents."

One afternoon Mrs Ronald died while riding in the Daimler. Consequently in 1934 Elms Lea had to be sold so the estate could be shared between the children. Sadly the house was demolished, and the site redeveloped as housing, now Elms Lea Avenue.

Tivoli

Plans were drawn up in 1900 by E J Hamilton of New Road Brighton, for a house on the site of Tivoli Gardens for Mr W R Hawkins. It was finally erected in 1903, a year after its neighbour to the south, Tower House, which already occupied half the site of the Tivoli Gardens. Originally called Shalimar, the house was renamed Tivoli in the 1920's. In 1929 it was bought by Mr Thomas Price who owned Price's Bakery in Coombe Road and had shops in Bond Street and East Street. He lived at Tivoli with his wife and son until the late 30's and is remembered for staging a two day party at the house for his son's twenty first birthday. The house was compulsorily purchased by Brighton Council and became one of its Welfare Services Residential Homes. The family moved to 'Merok' in Dyke Road Avenue and later sold their bakery to Forfars. Tivoli was demolished in 1988 and is now the site of the Tower Gate flats.

Tivoli in the 1930s, home of T W Price of Price's bakeries.

Tower House

Tower House, was built on about half the site of Tivoli Gardens, and is Brighton's finest example of a grand Edwardian house. It was designed by G Burstow & Sons for James John Savage for his retirement in 1902. Mr Savage's wanted a house with a tower, which would offer panoramic views over the surrounding neighbourhood. The family monogram and date can still be seen above the front door. James Savage was a jeweller by royal appointment to Edward VII, had lived and worked in London for many years before moving to Brighton with his wife Elizabeth Ellen, and daughters Mabel, Connie & Elsie.

The Savages were a sociable family and their house contained all the necessary rooms for living in traditional Edwardian style. There were three maids, a cook and a gardener/chauffeur, most of whom lived in the house. The family were musical, and Mr Savage took a personal interest in the Brighton School of Music in Preston Road, where he presented a gold medal for composition. In addition to reception rooms, living rooms and servants quarters, Tower House also had a billiard room, and a conservatory. The imposing entrance hall was illuminated by daylight through a stained glass ceiling; with a grand staircase rising from the centre and dividing in two, and running the full width of the galleried landing. The house had been equipped with a number of features unusual for their day, which included an under-floor heating system with pipes giving out heat through gratings, and a bathroom in which one end of the bath was fitted with a shower.

Mr Savage died in 1922 aged 75. Mrs Savage remained at Tower House until her death aged 81 in 1933. She had been a woman of personality who had contributed to many charities. At the outbreak of war in 1914, she and a few of her friends formed a social sewing party for the benefit of the soldiers and their families. On more than one occasion, Tower House and its large grounds were thrown open for charitable garden parties.

Tower House was sold at auction in 1934 for the sum of £4000, The sale details describe the house as having 'Eight principal bed and dressing rooms, four secondary bedrooms, three bathrooms, four reception rooms, spacious hall, billiard room, compact domestic offices, garage, conservatory and outbuildings in two acres of delightful grounds affording selusion and screen from the road'. It was bought by Mr A C Berryman who with his wife and four daughters had lived in India for some years and upon their return to England had settled at Norbury (now the Jarvis Preston Park Hotel). However when widening of London Road was proposed, resulting in the loss of much of their front garden, the family moved to Tower House. One of the daughters, Mrs. Merle Meyer continued to live there for many years. During the Second World War, Tower House was requisitioned by the ATS, but reverted its original use as a private house in 1946.

In 1988, Tower House and the remaining grounds, were acquired from the owner Miss Milldred Hooker, by Cussins Green Homes. The refurbishment of the house and its conversion into flats on the upper floors and tower, with a resource centre on the ground floor, necessitated the removal of the staircase and the stained glass ceiling in the hall. The exterior of the house has been restored to its original appearance, including the weather vane on top of the tower. The remaining grounds, along with those of the demolished Tivoli House next door, now accommodate the Robinia Lodge flats in Station Road, newly built blocks of flats called Towergate, and an adjacent terrace of houses.

Opposite: Tower House in 1939, built in 1902 for J J Savage on the site of Tivoli Gardens.

Merle Meyer outside Tower House in 1939.

The back garden of Tivoli in 1928, facing west.

Below Stairs in the Withdean Villas

The houses in this survey comprise mansions for the very wealthy to relatively modest (by Victorian standards) villas for lower paid professional men and women. At the top end of the scale was Withdean Court, built by Clayton and Black in 1871 for Elizabeth, Lady Ogle, widow of Sir Charles Ogle. The 1871 census shows a staff consisting of a secretary, lady's maid, cook, two housemaids, and a footman; ten years later there was a cook, upper housemaid, housemaid, kitchenmaid, footman, and a living-in coachman. A cowman and a gardener lived above the cowshed in the grounds. Oddly, no butler is recorded in either census return; he may have been absent on census day.

Laine House was considerably smaller but the 1871 census returns record that Mary and her husband William Wooldridge, a non practising general practitioner living on income from investments, were supported by a cook, housemaid, housekeeper and coachman. Curiously, the housekeeper, Rebecca Fleet, was living in the gardener's cottage on census day. Laine House had no basement offices; the ground plan[1] shows a kitchen, pantry, scullery and attached store room. The house falls into the category described by Stefan Muthesius[2] as belonging to the prosperous professional man. There was no servants' staircase, butler's department or servants' hall. The servants' living room was the kitchen.

Ten years after it was built in 1861, Withdeane Hall was, according to the 1871 census, occupied by Susan Lacy, a seventy-nine year old widow. Her staff consisted of a lady's maid, butler, cook and housemaid together with a coachman and his wife living above the coach house and a gardener with his wife and daughter living in the gardener's cottage. By 1881 the house was occupied by Frank Mowatt, a principal clerk in the Treasury. He and his wife had six children (and one step-son) and a staff consisting of a German governess and her maid, a lady's maid, cook, two housemaids, two nursemaids, a kitchenmaid, butler and footman.

Tower House, Withdean, built in 1902, had seventeen rooms and what were described as 'compact domestic offices' in two acres of grounds.[3] The census returns of this house are unavailable but in the will of Elizabeth Savage of Tower House dated 16 February 1934 bequests were made to the gardener, cook, chauffeur (who may well have been a former coachman) and an unspecified number of maids. Muthesius describes seventeen-roomed houses, excluding the servants' offices, as belonging to that section of society which overlapped with the upper class. It consisted of the 200,000 families of lawyers, merchants and top civil servants earning between £1,000 and £3,000 per annum.[4]

In contrast to these mansions were the houses which formerly flanked Preston Road opposite Preston Park. Numbers 125-139 Preston Road consisted of semi-detached villas built by Messrs Holloway of Brighton in 1877. These houses had seven bedrooms (including servants' bedrooms) and three reception rooms. The basement offices consisted of a kitchen, scullery, housekeeper's room and butler's pantry leading to a beer and wine cellar, coal cellar and boot house (for cleaning shoes). As at Laine House, the kitchen would have functioned as a servants' hall and although a butler's pantry is mentioned, it would almost certainly have been used by a maidservant.[5]

Considerably larger were the detached villas at number 161 and 163 Preston Road. These were designed by the Brighton architect J. Thomas in 1875 and consisted of eight bedrooms, three reception rooms (a through drawing room, a dining room and a library)

Servants beating carpets at Effingham Lodge in 1929. Left to right: Mrs Wagstaff, the cook; Mr Bull, the gardener; and a maid.

and basement offices which included a kitchen, scullery, servery, and pantry. Interestingly, there was a basement breakfast room. This was rather old-fashioned for the date and was added, usually to smaller houses, when the dining room was inadequate.[6]

Common to all these houses was a sub-division of function which aimed to provide minimum interruption to the family from their servants. It was a Victorian article of faith that the family should not trespass upon the servants' territory and the servants' offices were so arranged that specific functions were allocated to specific rooms. Of course, in smaller houses the ideal as exemplified in Robert Kerr's *The Gentleman's House*, 1864, tended to break down in the face of practical necessity. For example, the kitchen might function as a servants' hall. Nevertheless, privacy and separation were essential for men and women servants and their working areas were separate, the only common meeting place being the servants' hall or, in smaller houses, the kitchen. This was not normally a problem as male staff were rare because they cost more and were taxed, unlike female staff. The only male staff in the larger houses under consideration would have been a butler, footman, gardener and coachman. In the smaller villas the entire staff would have been female, although occasionally a single footman was kept.

The butler was the senior male servant. He was responsible for the silver, wine and beer, and waiting at meals. His pantry was close to the housekeeper's room, the dining room and the cellars. In a substantial house, such as Withdeane Hall, he would have been assisted by a footman who, amongst other duties, would have cleaned the boots and shoes, filled the coal scuttles, trimmed the lamps, brushed the master's clothes and helped the butler wait at table. When out on carriage duty he gave directions to the coachman and carried messages.

The female analogue of the butler in the servants' hierarchy was the housekeeper who, again, would have been present only in the larger houses. She was distinguished by her symbol of office, a chatelaine of keys at her waist. The housekeeper was in charge of the china, the linen and all supplies except food for the kitchen. She engaged and dismissed all female staff except the cook and lady's maid. Her room functioned as an upper servants' common room and was always lined with cupboards for the storage of china and linen. The housekeeper rose at 7.30am (an hour later than the maids) and after breakfast with the upper servants she would check the work of the housemaids, inspect the bedrooms, and, in the afternoon, arrange dessert for dinner, prepare biscuits and cakes for tea and arrange tea and coffee in the drawing room after dinner.

The housemaids normally started work at 6.30am. Mrs Beeton in *The Book of Household Management* (1859-61) commented that 'earlier than this would probably be an unnecessary waste of coals and candles in winter'. Duties included opening the shutters, sweeping the breakfast room, and then laying the fires, blackleading the grates, dusting and polishing. 'It is not enough', commented Mrs Beeton, 'just to pass lightly over the surface; the rims and legs of tables, and the backs and legs of chairs and sofas, should be rubbed vigorously daily; if there is a bookcase, every corner of every pane and ledge requires to be carefully wiped, so that not a speck of dust can be found in the room.'[7] The stairs were then swept, the drawing room cleaned and the breakfast laid, after which the bedrooms were aired, the bedclothes removed, the slops emptied and the beds made. Mrs Beeton describes bed-making in minute detail, commenting, for instance, that 'any feathers which escape in this process (turning the mattress) a tidy servant will put back through the seam of the tick'.[8]

The amount of work done by the housemaids depended, of course, upon the number of servants kept. Where there were no parlourmaids or footmen the silver, for instance, would still have to be cleaned. Various weekly works were also prescribed, these included brushing mattresses, taking down the curtains, scrubbing the floors, and polishing the looking glasses. Evening duties consisted of laying-out night clothes and lighting the bedroom fires in the winter. The housemaids were also expected to be able to do some needlework for the mistress. This constant round of work was in part due to the density of furnishings and the ubiquity of the coal fire with its concomitant dirt.

The kitchen was the most important of all the service rooms. Its planning had to be carefully considered because, as Robert Kerr commented,[9] 'the position of the Kitchen governs the arrangement of its accessories'. It had to relate to the larders and back entrance for supplies; to the scullery for cleaning; to the dining room and to the servants' hall. The Victorians had a horror of cooking smells and as much nineteenth-century cooking consisted of roasting in front of the fire it is perhaps unsurprising that the novelist Mary Cholmondeley referred to them in 1897 as 'evil, subtle, nauseous and overpowering'.[10] The dinner route had to be planned so that the transmission of odours to the dining room was carefully guarded against. This often meant that there was a somewhat circuitous route from the kitchen and that food could arrive cold. Disraeli was once heard to murmur when the champagne arrived, 'Thank God for something warm'.[11] This sensitivity to kitchen smells may seem exaggerated but when it is remembered how many dishes were prepared and that Mrs Beeton in 1861 recommended that cabbage should be boiled for up to three quarters of an hour, it is perhaps not unreasonable to liken the smell of the kitchen in a large Victorian house to a school dining room today.

Fittings varied according to the size of the kitchen but pride of place was taken by the cast iron close range, also known as a kitchener. Occasionally an open range would also have been provided for roasting. A boiler was normally provided at the back of the range. There might also have been a stewing stove heated by charcoal, a hot-plate, a hot-closet and a hot-table. The kitchen dresser had shelves which housed the *batterie de cuisine* of copper cooking utensils. These were highly valued and were cleaned, by the scullerymaid, with silver sand and vinegar. The interiors were tinned in order to avoid verdigris poisoning. As the tin could not be sanded for fear of scratching the coating, the inside had to be soaked with water and cleaned with a cloth.

Inside the kitchen the cook was dominant; Mrs Beeton referred to her as 'queen of the kitchen'. Sometimes, even in large houses, the position of cook and housekeeper were combined and her duties were thus particularly onerous. But it was in the preparation of dinner that the cook's skills were put to the test. 'Then comes haste', commented Mrs Beeton, 'but there must be no hurry - all must work with method'.[12] Cooks' perks included bones, dripping and fat, all of which could be sold.

Adjoining the kitchen was the scullery which was used for washing and cleaning dishes and preparing fish, game and vegetables. It was regarded as essential that the washing of dirty vessels was kept apart from the work of the kitchen. Fixtures usually included a pair of sinks, one made of stoneware, the other of wood lined with lead, a table, a plate-rack placed above the sink with a drip-board, and, in larger houses, a boiling copper for kitchen cloths. In smaller houses the scullery might function as a place of all work, washing especially included. Nearby, again depending on the size of the house, there might be a cook's pantry where cold meats, bread, milk and butter were stored, and a meat larder or wet larder for uncooked meats, vegetables or fruit.

In smaller houses, as we have seen, the kitchen might function as the servants' day room. At Tower House or Withdean Court there would have been a separate servants' hall. It was classed amongst the lower servants' offices whereas the housekeeper's room and butler's pantry were upper servants' rooms. The room was planned so that it was close to the kitchen and the upper servants' rooms. Although some upper servants ate meals here, it primarily functioned as the dining room of the lower servants and the waiting room for all persons ranked with the lower servants. Robert Kerr recommended that it ought to have a prospect 'which shall be at least not disagreeable; the outlook, however, ought not to be towards the walks of the family'.[13] Fittings included a table for meals, side tables or a dresser, pin-rails for hats, a set of Windsor chairs or, more usually, benches, china cupboards, and essentially, a clock. It was quite normal to furnish the servants' hall with old-fashioned furniture from the family rooms and even, in larger houses, portraits of out of favour ancestors of the family. Religious prints and texts were also often provided to encourage a high moral tone. In smaller houses the servants' hall had many incidental purposes - brushing clothes, ironing, even serving dinner and washing up. It was the only servants' recreation room and the only area where the sexes could legitimately meet.

Male and female servants slept in different areas of the house. Female servants normally had attic bedrooms whereas male servants frequently slept in airless and stuffy basement rooms. Two maidservants might share a bedroom but male lower servants commonly had their own rooms. Upper servants (the cook, housekeeper and butler) always had their own bedrooms. Fittings were plain and simple: a cast iron bed, a chest of drawers, a washstand, a chair and a towel horse were quite usual.

The plan of even a moderately sized Victorian house aimed to provide efficiently run service rooms. Robert Kerr wrote: 'the Family Apartments have to be contrived for residence; but the offices for work ... in the Family Rooms the problem is how to make them most comfortable and pleasant; in the Offices it is rather how to dispose of everything for facility of business'.[14] Even before 1914 the emphasis on subdivision of function and rigid segregation had begun to break down and today, in those few Withdean villas that survive, the service areas have been altered beyond recognition. In their heydey, however, they must have presented an impression of well-organized activity with largely invisible servants ministering to the family's every need. [References inside back cover]

David Beevers

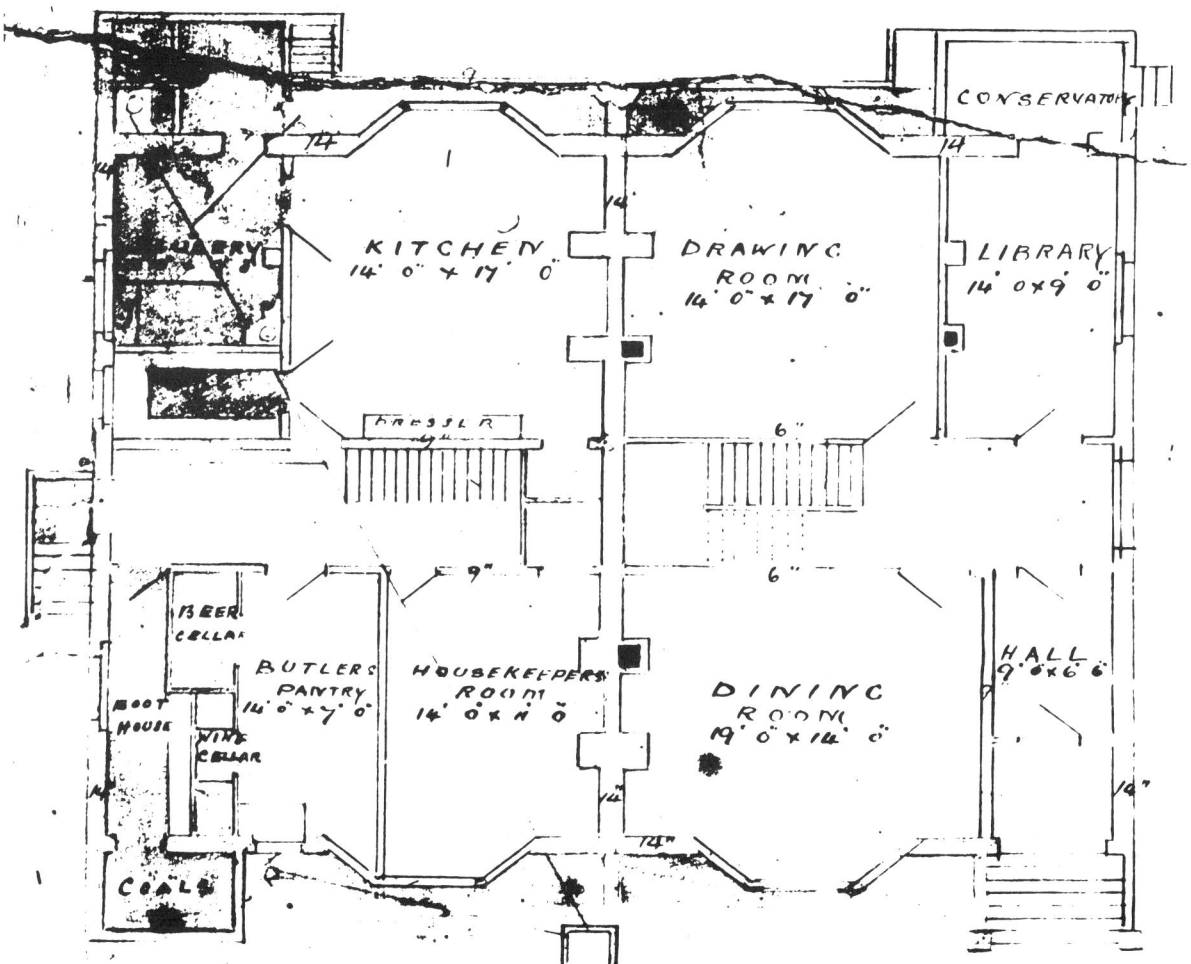

Plan of basement and ground floor of semi-detached villas nos 125-139 Preston Road

Rossmore - 127 Preston Road (see front cover)

Rossmore, built in 1878 by Messrs Holloway of Brighton, was half of one of the four pairs of large semi-detached houses built along Preston Road opposite the end of Stanford Avenue. The four storey houses were set back from the road with a basement consisting of a kitchen, scullery, housekeeper's room and butler's pantry as well as cellars and a WC. The ground floor consisted a drawing room, dining room, library and conservatory, while the first floor had three bedrooms and a bathroom and WC. The attic was divided into four bedrooms for the servants. The house remained in private occupation, although in multiple occupancy from the 1930's, and was unlisted in the street directories after the early 1970's. The British Telecom offices now stand on this site.

Springcroft - 163 Preston Road

Springcroft was a larger detached villa designed by the Brighton architect J Thomas in 1875. It consisted of eight bedrooms, a drawing room, dining room, library and a basement area for the servants as well as stabling in the garden.

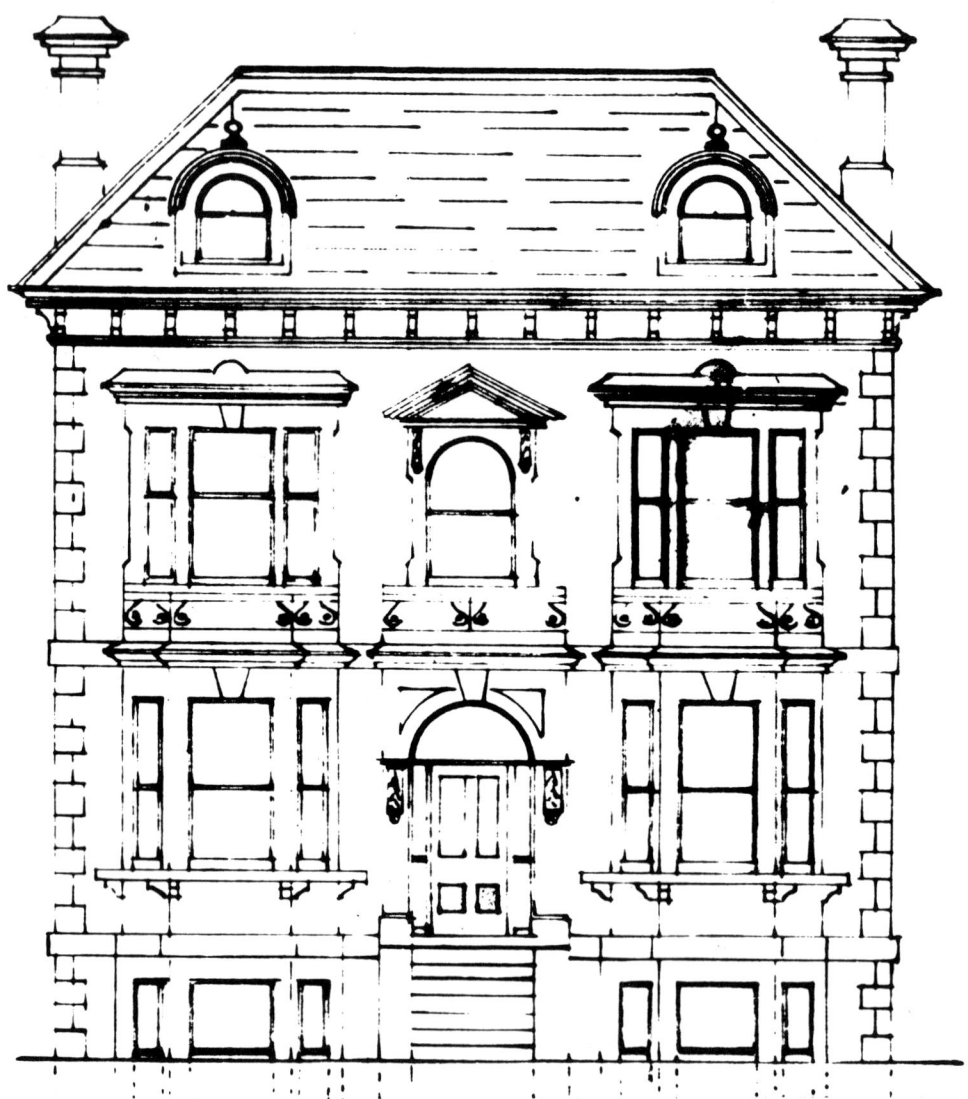

Architect's drawing for Springcroft, 163 Preston Road.

Mr. Alfred Jones remembers his father talking about his grandfather's life as a coachman at Springcroft just before the World War I.

"My father Charles Jones, was born above the stable at Springcroft in Preston Road. His father Albert Jones was the coachman to the family and his mother Maria was the cook. There were three girls and four boys in the family and all nine of them lived in the two rooms above the stables. One room was used for general living and the other as a bedroom for his parents and the three daughters. The four boys slept together in the hayloft and through the cracks in the floor could see the six horses stabled below.

Architect's drawing for the stable block of 163 Preston Road.

Dad and his brothers had to leave the house early in the morning and not return until later in the day as the owner did not want to see urchins around his property.

Like many other men of that era, my grandfather drunk quite heavily on occasions and it was quite usual for the gentlemen of the houses in the Preston area to go to the 'lock up' on Sunday morning and bail out their coachmen in order to be driven to church.

The lady of the house liked to hack but unfortunately was killed while out riding. The master married a younger wife who wanted a car rather than a horse and carriage, and tried to persuade my grandfather to learn to drive. When he was given the money to pay for driving lessons he drank it away rather than have lessons, only waking up after he had enlisted in the army veterinary corps! He served all through the 1914-18 war, returning to Preston to work for Mr Pritchard, a vet who lived at the end of Clermont Road. Opposite Mr. Pritchard's house was a house called Grove Lodge where a Dr Simpson lived. He delivered most of the children in Preston at that time and he assisted at my birth at a laying-in house at 23 Robertson Road, 70 years ago."

The house remained in private occupation until the late 1930's when it became offices for the Automobile Association and in the 1960's and 70's Cornhill Insurance.

The Grove - 167 Preston Road

The Grove was a large detached house built in the 1870's, situated just south of Lovers Walk. It was a private residence until the 1970's although often in multiple occupancy after the World War II. Ruby Dunn remembers living there after her husband was invalided out of the army in February 1946.

"My husband and I lived at 167 Preston Road from February 1946 until Spring 1949. We had no home and very little money, and were grateful to be offered the first floor flat by a friend, who had bought the property in a somewhat derelict state at a low price. There was some evidence of structural faults and doors were ill-fitting. This may have been as a result of the bombing of the Preston Viaduct during the war. A gate in Lover's Walk gave access to garages at the rear of the property that had once been the stabling for the horses and carriage. The garden flower beds, shrubberies and the summer house were a pleasure. Next door to us was a similar house with additions at the rear called Preston College. It functioned as a school for years after we left. When we left our first home it was not so much by choice but by persuasion. We were sad to hear of the demolition of all those fine houses to make way for the present monstrosities."

During the 1950's and 60's, many of the houses in Preston Road became run down. After a series of tenants The Grove became offices for Preece Cardew & Rider, consulting engineers before its demolition. Paston House now stands on the site.

Montrose 173 Preston Road in 1910, typical of the detached villas facing Preston Park.

Montrose - 173 Preston Road

Montrose was typical of the large detached villas in Preston Road. Situated three houses north of Lover's walk and built in the 1870's in spacious grounds, it was lived in for many years by the Leeson family. Next door, the identical villa 'Carisbrooke' was lived in by Joseph Sykes and his wife and daughter Josephine. On her twenty first birthday a section of Preston Park was hired to give a tea to selected poor people of the town. After World War II Montrose remained in private occupation until the sixties when it became the offices of the Sussex Territorial & Auxiliary Forces Association. By the 1970's it was empty. Carisbrooke became the home of the Flinn family during the 1920's but was known as 'Carisbrooke School' during the 1930's. After World War II it first became Preston College Nursery School and then Preston Park Nursery School. In the late 60's it was used as the Confederation Life Assurance of Canada offices, but was demolished in the early seventies. Today H M Inspector of Taxes has offices on the site.

The Downs School - 183-185 Preston Road

Originally built as two semi-detached houses opposite the gates of Preston Park, by 1907 they were jointly used as a girls' school called 'The Downs' and run by the Misses Charlton & Cooper. Miss Watts remembers that her mother attended this school as a boarder between the dates 1910-14 She remembered the Misses Cooper who wore long rustling skirts, high necked blouses, waistcoats and necklaces. The girls used Preston Park and played in the bushes where the Blind Garden is today and visited the chalet which sold stale cakes under glass covers and 1d bars of chocolate.

From the 1920's until the late 30's the school was run by the Misses Woodhead & Cleare but by 1938 it had closed and had been converted to 12 flats called Nestor Court. By 1968 the building was empty and derelict and being used by 'beatniks and tramps' according to the Evening Argus. Local people were relieved to see it demolished but it was a sad end of a once thriving school. Today the site contains blocks of flats called Nestor Court and the offices of Unison.

Above: view of the garden from the balcony of the Downs School, Preston Road.

Above: Vista looking north of the Preston Park villas, 129-151 Preston Road in 1959.

'Beyond [Patcham] is a stretch of road and gritty pathways leading to the welcome shade of Withdean trees, and in another mile, diversified now with many villas, and dusty and gritty beyond mere words, is Preston.

Preston turnpike gate erected about 1807, was removed in May 1854 to a point a 100 yards north of Withdean, as the result of an agitation started in 1853, when the Highway Trustees were applying to parliament for another term of years. It and its hateful legend 'No Trust' painted large for all the world to see, were a nuisance and a gratuitous satire upon human nature, no one regretted them when their time came.'

The Brighton Road by Charles G Harper 1892